TOUCHING

by Robin Nelson

first step nonfiction

Lerner Publications Company · Minneapolis

Touch is one of my **senses.**

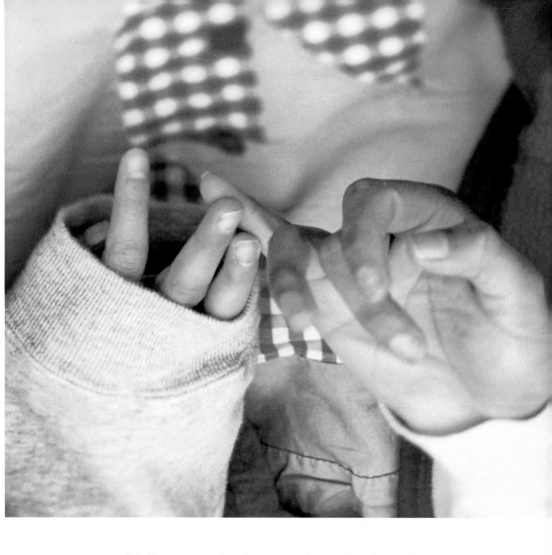

When I touch, I feel
with my **skin.**

3

I feel something hard.
I feel a shell.

I feel a bat.

5

I feel something soft.
I feel a blanket.

6

I feel fur.

I feel something **smooth.**
I feel a slide.

I feel paint.

I feel something **rough.**
I feel a **pinecone.**

I feel a tree.

I feel something hot.
I feel sand in the sun.

I feel bath water.

I feel something cold.
I feel snow.

I feel ice cream.

I touch many things.

What do you feel?

nerves

How do you feel?

You feel things with your skin.

You have special nerves in

your skin. When you touch

something, your nerves send

a message to your brain.

Then your brain figures out

what you are touching.

Touching Facts

 The skin is the largest organ of the body.

 You have more pain nerve endings than any other type.

 The most sensitive areas of your skin are your hands, lips, face, neck, tongue, fingertips, and feet. Your fingertips are the most sensitive part of your body.

 The least sensitive part of your skin is the middle of your back.

There are about 100 nerve endings in each of your fingertips.

 Touch is a very important sense. Babies who are not touched, stroked, kissed, held, and cuddled are less healthy than babies who are touched.

 Our sense of touch keeps us safe. When we feel heat, cold, or pain we move away from it.

Glossary

 pinecone – the seeds of a pine tree

 rough – does not feel even

 senses – the five ways our bodies get information. The five senses are hearing, seeing, smelling, tasting, and touching.

 skin – the outer covering on human and animal bodies

 smooth - feels even

Index

Cover image used courtesy of: Brand X Pictures.

Photos reproduced with the permission of: Corbis Royalty Free Images, pp. 2, 9, 13, 22 (middle); Brand X Pictures, pp. 3, 16, 22 (second from bottom); © Frances M. Roberts, p. 4; © Brian Vikander/CORBIS, p. 5; © Michael S. Yamashita/CORBIS, p. 6; © RubberBall Royalty Free Digital Stock Photography, p. 7; © Kit Kittle/CORBIS, pp. 8, 22 (bottom); © Betty Crowell, pp. 10, 22 (top, second from top); © G. Hofstetter/Photo Network, p. 11; © Elaine Little/World Photo Images, p. 12; © David A. Jentz/Photo Network, p. 14; © David Bartuff/CORBIS, p. 15; © Stockbyte, p. 17.

Illustration on page 18 by Tim Seeley.

Lerner Publications Company
A division of Lerner Publishing Group
241 First Avenue North
Minneapolis, MN 55401 U.S.A.

Website address: www.lernerbooks.com

Library of Congress Cataloging-in-Publication Data

Nelson, Robin, 1971–
    Touching / by Robin Nelson.
        p. cm. — (First step nonfiction)
    Includes index.
    Summary: An introduction to the sense of touch and the
different things that you can feel.
    ISBN: 0–8225–1266–1 (lib. bdg. : alk. paper)
    1. Touch—Juvenile literature. [1. Touch. 2. Senses and
sensation.] I. Title. II. Series.
QP451 .N45 2002
612.8'8—dc21   2001003963

Manufactured in the United States of America
1 2 3 4 5 6 – AM – 07 06 05 04 03 02